Original title:

Sands of Solitude

Copyright © 2025 Creative Arts Management OÜ

All rights reserved.

Author: Alec Donovan

ISBN HARDBACK: 978-1-80581-559-4

ISBN PAPERBACK: 978-1-80581-086-5

ISBN EBOOK: 978-1-80581-559-4

Traces of Breath on the Untouched Sand

In the dunes where whispers play,
A daring squirrel leads the way.
He slips and slides, what a scene,
Who knew nuts could dance so keen?

Footprints left by moonlit mice,
Sketching mischief, oh so nice!
While crabs in tuxedos strut,
They wave their claws, who needs a hut?

Embracing Shadows in the Cosmic Stillness

Stars above have taken flight,
While shadows groove, a comical sight.
They bounce and sway like floppy hats,
Who knew the dark had such chitchats?

With twinkling light as laughter's tune,
Even the owls are startin' to croon.
Mystic vibes in a wacky show,
Who knew silence had such flow?

The Ascent to Quietude Among Stones

Rocks are piled, a jumbled stack,
One says, 'Let's plan an attack!'
They roll their eyes, they crack a joke,
Even boulders share a poke.

A pebble grumbles, 'Not so fast!'
While granite shouts, 'We'll never last!'
Up to heights of giggly glee,
Who knew cliffs could hold a spree?

Navigating the Depths of Isolation

In a nook where whispers hide,
A goldfish dreams of a wild ride.
He flops and flails, with great delight,
'Can I join the seagulls in flight?'

The lonely cactus tries to quirk,
Telling tales to lizards at work.
But they laugh and say, 'You're too prickly!'
Isolation's fun, oh so tickly!

Mirage of Loneliness in the Distant Light

A cactus danced with glee, so bright,
While tumbleweeds rolled out of sight.
The sun wore shades, quite absurd,
And whispered secrets, not a word.

The sand said, "Hey, I'll tell you a joke!"
But laughter vanished, like smoke.
With each footstep, echoes of fun,
Chasing shadows under the sun.

The Erosion of Lost Connections

Once I called a lizard friend,
But he was late, a worldly trend.
The wind just chuckled, blew it away,
While I sat alone, come what may.

Vultures watched from their high thrones,
While I picked up my forgotten phone.
No signal found, it laughed in mirth,
Unplugged from life, my own little blurt.

Beneath the Quiet Surface of Time

Tick tock laughed the lazy clock,
As I sank in time's ticklish rock.
Each grain a joke, a punchline missed,
While laughter lingered in the mist.

With every hour, a giggle grows,
But there I stand, with my toes in prose.
Time created a funny little mess,
And I wondered, 'Is this my best?'

Whispered Stories in the Desert Night

In the darkness, the stars would tease,
With ancient tales that never freeze.
A rabbit waltzed beneath the moon,
While the owls hooted a lonely tune.

'Let's play hide and seek!' they claimed,
But in the vastness, no one was named.
Their laughter echoed, a ghostly fright,
In whispered stories of the night.

Fragments of Time along a Silent Path

Ticking clocks in a quiet space,
Pigeons plotting their next big race.
Grass grows wild, oh what a sight,
As squirrels hold meetings in daylight.

Old shadows dance with gentle cheer,
While the breeze whispers jokes in my ear.
Laughter echoes with each gentle breeze,
Amid the rustling of the trees.

Echoing Hours in an Empty Realm

In a realm where whispers play,
Tickle the cactus, what do they say?
Time floats by on a sleepy cloud,
While ants break ground, feeling quite proud.

Old boots left behind on the trail,
Chasing memories, how funny the tale!
Dust devils whirl like dervishes bold,
As secrets, they keep, are better than gold.

Tides of Reflection on the Desert Floor

Mirrors of mirage fool the eye,
As tumbleweeds aim for the sky.
Laughing lizards join in a dance,
In this dry place, they take a chance.

With each twist and turn upon the ground,
Echoes of humor in silence found.
Jumping jackrabbits leap with flair,
While the sun blinks back with a nonchalant stare.

The Heartbeat of Remote Places

Distant echoes of a chuckling stream,
Where rocks conspire and sunbeams gleam.
Lonely turtles move with such grace,
In a race that's at a leisurely pace.

Mountains giggle, the valleys reply,
As clouds float by, puffed up with pride.
Nature's laughter in every bend,
A quiet joke that will never end.

Waves of Dunes Against the Silent Sky

Dunes that dance under a bright sun,
Laughter erupts, it's all in good fun.
Footprints vanish, like socks in the wash,
A mirage tumbles, quite the harmless swash.

From camels that giggle at silly hats,
To seagulls that steal your hungry snacks.
Breezes blow whispers to tickle your ears,
While sand makes a castle, fueled by your cheers.

Reflections in an Untrodden Landscape

Mirror-like puddles in endless terrain,
Where shadows play tricks, driving you insane.
You leap to escape, but trip on a rock,
And splash in a puddle — oh, what a shock!

Unseen critters clap, as you scramble to rise,
Cacti look on with their curious eyes.
The sun tries to roast you, but it can't find a way,
For laughter's the spice in this ridiculous play.

Secrets Buried Beneath Shifting Layers

Beneath the soft earth, where secrets are stored,
An old rubber chicken, quite well adored.
It giggles in silence, with tales to regale,
Of tumbled adventures that always prevail.

Shovels dig deep, like dreams out of reach,
Finding a sandwich — oh, life's quirky screech!
Each grain of sand, a giggle to share,
As treasure hunters stumble with leaps and a flair.

When Winds Weep for the Untamed

Winds howl like toddlers, in a fit for a toy,
Tumbling the tumbleweeds — oh, what a joy!
They moan for the lost, then dance in full glee,
While tumble and roll like they're wild and free.

The cheeky breeze teases hats off your head,
Causes a dance, as though you're misled.
With each gust, a laugh, a comical fall,
In this wild and vast stretch, we're all in for a brawl.

Breath of the Withering Wind

The breeze has jokes, oh what a thrill,
It whispers secrets, but won't stand still.
It tickles my nose, then runs away,
Laughing at me, 'You can't make me stay!'

Each tumbleweed rolls like a ball of yarn,
Chasing the dust with a cheeky charm.
They weave through shadows, take a wild spin,
In this featherweight dance, let the fun begin!

Conversations with the Distant Sun

Hey there, Sun, you think you're so bright,
But I caught you snoozing at midday's height!
Your rays are blazing, yes, we all see,
But don't you forget who's got the best tea!

You wink and you grin, with a golden sigh,
While clouds roll in, like a fluffy pie.
You tease and you flirt, but when I'm on fire,
You cool off quick, running from the choir!

Nightfall Over the Silent Expanse

The moon broke in, with a goofy grin,
Claiming my slice and twirling within.
Stars giggle softly, they wink in delight,
'Look at the earthling, all scared of the night!'

Owls in the trees sing a sweet lullaby,
While shadows are dancing, oh my, oh my!
Crickets are drummers with legs made for jazz,
In the cool stillness, they throw a big razz!

Reflections in a Grainy Mirror

Just caught my glance in a dusty pane,
My hair's in a tussle, a beautiful bane.
The face smirks back, a wild, funny sprite,
'Who dressed you today, a raccoon in the night?'

I laugh with my shadow, we jest and we joke,
It's a carnival fun house, and oh what a poke!
Life's but a riddle, a slapstick affair,
In this grainy mirror, we dance without care!

Whispers of the Desert Breezes

In the dunes, a lizard plays,
Cactus hats on sunny days.
With a tiny dance, he twirls,
Giving shade to passing girls.

Cacti gossip, ever sly,
Wearing sombreros, oh so spry.
A tumbleweed rolls by and winks,
Laughing softly as it thinks.

Sandstorms howl, but they just laugh,
Missing the punchline of a giraffe.
Every grain with a jolly cheer,
Makes the world feel light, my dear.

So let the breezes share their jokes,
With every sway and twist, it pokes.
For in the heat, a wink and grin,
Turns the boring into a win.

Echoes in the Abandoned Dunes

Once a caravan, now a plot,
A ghostly rider with a thought.
His camel scoffs, all ears aglow,
As they search for a place to go.

Footsteps echo, but they tease,
"Did you forget your map, dear please?"
Laughter dances in their wake,
Like a mirage, a funny mistake.

Wind whispers tales of clumsy pairs,
Trying to pitch tents in swirling airs.
With every flop, they just can't hide,
Their laughter ripples with desert pride.

Hidden details in the haze,
Make the desert sing in funny ways.
Look closer, find the jester's game,
Life's too short to feel the same.

Mirage of Silent Dreams

In the distance, a well so bright,
Filled with lemonade, pure delight.
But the jar of joy always sways,
Leaving thirsty dreamers in a daze.

A ghostly fox plays hide and seek,
In sand that sings when it's at its peak.
His jokes are earthy, but quite clever,
In mirage lands where light is never.

Beneath the stars, a pun takes flight,
A scorpion's grin under the moonlight.
Tickling thoughts of silly ways,
To pass the time during long days.

So grab your friends and start a feast,
For here, the humorous never ceased.
In playful whispers and silly schemes,
Life's a laugh in this realm of dreams.

The Solitary Oasis

A palm tree sways, a lazy joke,
While a frog croaks a tale bespoke.
Here, the coconuts wear cool shades,
Winking at all the sunblock raids.

Water glistens like a mirage screen,
It tickles toes in a playful sheen.
As tourists trip on sandy floors,
Each fall inspired by funny scores.

A lone duck quacks a silly tune,
While sipping juice from a silver spoon.
His friends are pineapples, all in place,
Rocking sunglasses with a goofy grace.

So come along this funky spot,
Where laughter bubbles—give it a shot.
In the quiet of a playful scene,
Life's a giggle, sweet and serene.

Cracks in the Vastness

Beneath the sun's relentless heat,
Lizards dance on tiny feet.
I try to count each little grain,
But half my fingers start to strain.

A cactus wears a silly hat,
Winking at the passing cat.
I laugh at all the lonesome sights,
As tumbleweeds take moonlit flights.

Ghosts of Roving Minds

Wandering spirits float and glide,
Lost in thoughts they cannot hide.
They giggle at the sunburnt knoll,
While I bumble like a rolling bowl.

Ideas drift like wayward items,
Joking 'bout their fiery whims.
In the quiet, weird ideas prance,
As visions jiggle, laugh, and dance.

A Canvas of Eternal Dust

In a realm that's dull and dry,
I painted clouds with silly sighs.
Each brushstroke whimsically blue,
To surprise the cacti, just a few.

The dust bunnies do a grand parade,
In flowy gowns that never fade.
They twirl and leap around so spry,
While I watch and let out a sigh.

The Solitary Mirage

Out in the heat, I see a prior,
A drink that's cold, my heart's desire.
But all I find is pixel-steep,
Just a mirage making me weep.

Invisible friends join the fun,
They sip from cups, but there's just one.
I raise my glass to phantom cheers,
And laugh away my lonely fears.

Grains of Memory Caught in Time

A time traveler lost her shoe,
Chasing memories that just flew.
She trips on laughter, oh what a sight,
Dust clouds of giggles dance in the light.

Each grain, a tale of clumsy fun,
Stories twirl like a wild run.
With every stumble, she finds a clue,
A past so silly, how can it be true?

A sandcastle built, then washed away,
Like careers in "professional play."
She waves to waves with an awkward grin,
Life's a game, let the fun begin!

In the end, she takes a bow,
For every fumble made somehow.
These grains of laughter, they softly chime,
Forever caught in this silly time.

Solitude's Gaze on the Horizon

A hermit crab in a tiny shell,
Cracks jokes with seagulls, oh what the hell!
He gazes out at a vast blue sea,
Wondering if a friend will come for tea.

The sun is bright and so are his dreams,
Polka-dot crabs dance in silly beams.
With every wave, his muse takes flight,
In hearts of shells, there's so much delight.

He raises a cup to the flying fish,
Who promise to grant his every wish.
But they giggle and splash, diving about,
Friendship's flair, there's no doubt!

The horizon teases, holds secrets old,
Fish tales grow humorous and bold.
In solitude's gaze, he finds his cheer,
Life's a beach, with laughs ever near!

The Silent Song of Whispering Winds

The winds whisper secrets in a funny way,
They tickle the trees as they come out to play.
A riddle of gusts, oh what a tease,
Even the squirrels stop to sneeze!

Rustling leaves form a frolicsome tune,
Swaying like dancers beneath the moon.
In silent song, they share a jest,
Nature's humor, truly the best!

A breeze blows a hat off a nearby head,
With giggles and snorts, the crowd is led.
The wind laughs back, a whimsical sound,
As hats chase their owners around and around!

The echoes of wind play tricks so sly,
A flutter, a whistle, a joyful cry.
In silence they sing, those breezy friends,
With humor so light, that never ends.

Lonesome Echoes in the Twilight

In twilight's glow, the echoes run,
Chasing shadows, oh what fun!
A ghost said, "Boo!" with a silly grin,
It's hard to fear when you're laughing within!

The moon chuckles, all round and bright,
Making the stars twinkle with delight.
"What's a star do without a friend?"
"Shine brightly still, it's the latest trend!"

Echoes of laughter float through the night,
Calling for company, it feels so right.
A raccoon winks, and a coyote howls,
Together they weave enchanted growls.

As night wears on, the giggles resume,
With all this humor, who needs gloom?
In twilight's arms, they dance and sway,
Echoes of laughter lead the way!

A Serenade for the Forsaken Land

In a land so dry, the cactus wears shades,
For the sun's a jester, throwing hot escapades.
Lizards dance tango on a sunburned rock,
While tumbleweeds gossip, with time to mock.

Sipping on mirages, the oasis is sly,
Waving at travelers, as they pass by.
A lonesome jackrabbit sings a tune,
To the moon that chuckles, a cheeky buffoon.

The nights are quiet, but don't be misled,
The owls spin tales of the things that they dread.
A lost pair of socks just might start a fight,
In this place where dreams play hide-and-seek in the night.

So here's to the barren, the lonely and bold,
Where laughter is currency, far hotter than gold.
With echoes of fun in this sun-scorched land,
Let's raise a glass to the antics so grand.

Whispers of the Desert Wind

Oh, the wind tells secrets, so clever and sly,
It rustles the tumbleweeds, and causes a sigh.
"Watch out for the mirage with feet that can trip,"
It giggles and swirls like a half-empty sip.

In this vast expanse, the boulders conspire,
Deciding which cactus is most likely to fire.
Squeaky clean lizards, their tails in a twist,
Plot against the roadrunner, oh, don't be missed!

The stars up above are the flickering lights,
As camels play poker on starry nights.
With a deal and a bluff, they push all the chips,
And laugh at the way that the sun's got no quips.

So listen closely to the whispers around,
In this quirky expanse, silly jokes abound.
For in every gust there's a bit of delight,
Amidst dunes and shadows, the joy feels just right.

Echoes in the Empty Dunes

In the emptiness, echoes bounce off the sand,
As camels make friends, giving life to this land.
With each gentle roar, they gossip and play,
While the sun looks on, like it's judging the day.

A cactus stands tall, with a grin on its face,
It wears a straw hat, bringing style to this place.
The prickly debate 'tween the bugs and the flies,
Turns into a comedy under bright, open skies.

Lonely dunes giggle, shifting in jest,
Like they're sharing a punchline, this place is the best.
In a game of hide and seek, the shadows will hide,
But the sun can't resist, it simply won't bide.

So come join the laughter, the games in the heat,
Where footprints are jokes and they dance to the beat.
In the echoes of quiet, there's fun to be found,
In these rolling terrains, where silliness abound.

Solitary Footprints Beneath the Stars

A solitary footstep makes quite the affair,
As it whispers to starlight, "Is anyone there?"
The moon winks a joke, it's a curious night,
While crickets crack jokes that take lofty flight.

In this cosmic ballet, the shadows all sway,
Telling tales of the wanderers who lost their way.
A brave little ant, on a quest to be king,
Mocks at the stardust, while giggling it sings.

With each grain of sand, there's a story untold,
Of laughter and whimsy, both modern and old.
The breeze carries chuckles from far across lands,
As the footprints rejoice in the fun that expands.

So dance with the night, let the laughter ignite,
Under blankets of stars, what a magical sight.
For in solitude's grip, a party starts here,
With starlight and giggles, we'll banish the fear.

Forgotten Echoes of a Fractured Heart

In the attic of hearts, dust collects,
Old love letters hang like spider specs.
An old sock giggles from the corner,
While my heart sings tunes, a little foreigner.

Memories shuffle in mismatched shoes,
A dance of awkward, forgotten blues.
Each laugh is a ghost, a tickled grump,
While I trip on nostalgia, a lumpy lump.

The fridge hums, a lonely serenade,
In the spotlight, leftover pizza displayed.
I toast to the fumbles, a wine of regret,
In the theater of heartbreak, take your seat, a bet!

With every sip of my vintage surprise,
I learn to laugh, through the tears in my eyes.
In this comedy club where echoes reside,
I'll crack a few jokes while my hopes coincide.

The Solitary Watchtower's Vigil

A lone tower stands with a crooked hat,
Watching the world while I chase a cat.
Its snacks are stale, blown in the wind,
   Yet it still manages to wear a grin.

Patrolling the clouds like a restless guard,
Minds up in dreams, yet my own's still hard.
With pigeons as allies, we plot to conspire,
To catch every crumb that the world may require.

This lighthouse, a beacon for wayward minds,
   Cracks jokes about sailors and fishy finds.
Every sunset draws giggles from the past,
As it silently chuckles, a lighthouse cast.

I wave to the horizon, a playful salute,
For the lonely watchtower, it's quite a hoot.
In solitude's company, I'll take my cue,
   To laugh at the day, and start anew!

In the Company of Shadows Lost

Shadows bounce around like a clumsy dance,
Tripping over moonbeams in their dark, trance.
They whisper jokes with a phantom flair,
Offering puns that float in the air.

The lost ones giggle, a merry brigade,
Turning sorrows into a light masquerade.
With each passing hour, they play charades,
In the comedy club of forgotten parades.

Their laughter echoes, a haunting croon,
As I ponder my snack — a half-eaten moon.
In the twilight of whispers, they tease my heart,
Crafting a circus out of mundane art.

Together we wander past shadows and light,
In a world twisted funny, all feels just right.
Embracing the quirks, in this playful frost,
I find joy in the shadows, a love never lost.

Emptiness Worn like a Second Skin

Wrapped in the fabric of nothingness bold,
I wear my sorrow like a jacket of gold.
Pockets are empty, but still I walk tall,
With laughter as my armor, I'll stand through it all.

In this suit of vacuity, humor shines bright,
As punchlines and puns take off in flight.
The crickets join in with their own drum roll,
Wearing their silence like a jester's soul.

Each heartbeat a tick in a clock with no time,
Waltzing in circles, a whimsical rhyme.
Yet here, in this emptiness, I thrive and I grin,
For laughter does echo where no words have been.

With each little chuckle, I shed all my fears,
Donning my emptiness, spun with yarn of cheers.
In this fabric of solitude, I find my kin,
For joy's just a stitch away, waiting within.

Affirmation of a Solitary Pulse

In a crowded room, I sip my tea,
Talking to shadows, they listen to me.
My dance is a jig, quite out of sync,
A lively party, or was that just a blink?

I tell my reflection, we're quite the pair,
Debating our outfits, but who really cares?
With a wink to the mirror, I shuffle about,
The laughter inside me is what it's about.

Jokes with the wallpaper, a real delight,
It hangs there, so still, both day and night.
A joke about lemons, the punchline's a scream,
My one-woman show is a comical dream.

So here's to my pulse, all alone in this jig,
With each little giggle, I find my own dig.
I'll dance with my thoughts, till the end of my days,
In this quirky ballet, I'm lost in the blaze.

Unraveled Threads of Deserted Time

Tick-tock goes the clock, but no one is near,
I talk to my plants; they listen, I cheer.
A cactus with attitude, it's quite a sight,
I swear it rolled its eyes, but that can't be right.

My calendar's empty, like a donut's a hole,
With daydreams of trips, to a faraway pole.
I write letters to friends, they'll never receive,
Each one's a masterpiece, I'm hard to believe.

The sun kisses dust, and the dust just replies,
With a wink to the moon, and a slap at the flies.
Time has unraveled, like yarn on the floor,
A cat with a mission, it can't help but explore.

Between hearty giggles, I sip afternoon tea,
Stirring nothing but thoughts, just my friend and me.
So here's to lost moments, in laughter they bloom,
An echo in silence, a bulb in the gloom.

Chasing Ghosts in Shifting Tides

In a beach chair I sit, plot twists in the air,
Chasing shadows and whispers, do you see them? There!
A seagull just swooped, claiming a snack,
I wave to the ocean, but it won't wave back.

My bucket of dreams is all full of holes,
It spills all my laughter and half of my shoals.
I build a grand castle, it wobbles and melts,
A monument to joy, and the vibes that it dealt.

Each wave comes to tease, it splashes with glee,
I dodge like a ninja, oh look, there's a bee!
Ghosts in the surf, with their haunting hello,
They're just tidepools dancing in the sun's warm glow.

So I paddle my feet, in this playful ballet,
With laughter as my compass, I'll float through the day.
Chasing phantoms of joy, in this whimsical show,
Life's a giggle-fueled ride, and I'm ready to go.

Solstice of the Lonely Mirage

A mirage in the sun, with a twinkle and tease,
I wave to the breeze, it just chuckles with ease.
I'm searching for friends in this whimsical heat,
But it seems only tumbleweeds dance on their feet.

In the distance, I see a shimmering glow,
Is it a party, or just me? I don't know.
I follow the laughter, I'm nearly in tears,
It's just my own echo, dancing with fears.

My shadow plays tricks, it's an impish delight,
Doing the twist in the dim moonlight.
I pull out my sketchbook, to draw what I miss,
But all that I capture is a cartoonish bliss.

Yet here in the desert, I'm not really alone,
With mirages as pals, my humor has grown.
To the solstice of solitude, I now raise a cheer,
For in every silhouette, there's a friend standing near.

The Boundless Reach of Lonesome Stars

In the night, they twinkle bright,
But miss a friend to share the sight.
They shine alone in cosmic seas,
Wondering where the space geese please.

A star tried to make a witty joke,
But only comets laughed, then spoke.
With each wink, they silently compete,
For who can shine with the most beat.

From light-years away, they scream in glee,
Got no crowd, just me and me.
Yet in their glow, a chuckle hides,
Of solitude where humor rides.

So here they dance, in cosmic halls,
Drifting past with celestial brawls.
Alone they spin, but that's okay,
For even stars need a laugh today.

Carved Images in Solitary Stone

In a cave of echoes, rocks reside,
Whispering secrets, yet none confide.
Chiseled grins on every face,
Waiting for company to embrace.

A boulder slipped, it turned to laugh,
Called a pebble 'my better half.'
The stalactites join with gentle clinks,
Making puns while the granite winks.

Yet there they sit, unmoving, still,
Crafted with care, yet lacking thrill.
Oh, if these stones could only roam,
They'd build a party, call it home!

For every groove tells a jest or two,
In their solitude, laughter grew.
So let us toast to rocks alone,
Who need no audience for their tone.

The Eclipsed Light of Unshared Dreams

Beneath the night, a dream takes flight,
Yet lands on pillows with no delight.
An idea so bright, yet still it hides,
Waiting for others to share the rides.

A lone dreamer drew a silly frog,
Wishing for laughter, not just a slog.
Yet it hops around, inside the mind,
Only to find it's one of a kind.

With headlights beaming, thoughts collide,
But thoughts alone are hard to guide.
They ponder deep on jokes unsaid,
While shadows of clouds dance overhead.

So dreams, do sing in a silent cheer,
For humor thrives when friends are near.
Come join my whimsy, lend me your ear,
So laughter's light can finally appear!

Pathways Woven from Dust and Silence

In a world of wonder, dust will stray,
Crafting paths where none can play.
Footprints linger, but the laughs, they fade,
As silence settles in the glade.

A squirrel once tried to tell a tale,
But the winds whisked away the trail.
Dusty jokes formed a swirling dance,
But 'twas a solo, missed the chance.

Where trees bend low and shadows prance,
Laughter's seeds await their chance.
Yet still they drift on paths unseen,
In the quiet air, where sound's a dream.

So here I stand, in the gentle hush,
Hoping for friends to break the rush.
With every step, I'm set to laugh,
As dust and silence share their craft.

The Last Palms Standing

Under the sun's hot glare, they sway,
With fronds like fans, they laugh and play.
A toucan jokes, with beak so bright,
"You think you're cool? Just wait 'til night!"

Palm trees gossip, roots tangled tight,
Swapping tales of long-lost flights.
A breeze chuckles, tickles the leaves,
While the ground hides tricks that it weaves.

Beneath the shade, a lizard slips,
Eavesdropping on their verdant quips.
The sunburned guy with holiday tan,
Falls asleep, dreaming of a tan-less plan.

As evening falls, the stars align,
Each palm proclaims, "We've crossed the line!"
Staying strong, they won't retract,
The last palms standing, in laughter, intact.

Seclusion's Endless Expanse

A beach so wide, you can't find the end,
Seagulls tease, like an old, rough friend.
Lost flip-flops dance on the sand so fine,
  A crab rolls over, claiming it's mine!

Sunblock battles with the spray and mist,
"You missed a spot!" urges the sun's twist.
Meanwhile, umbrellas in chaos collide,
Windy antics giving no place to hide.

Out at sea, a boat drifts by,
With a captain shouting, "Why's the sky so shy?"
Fish laugh quietly, in bubbles they play,
While dolphins chuckle, swimming away.

In distant dunes, shadows perform,
Making shapes that twist and warm.
Seclusion's not lonely, it's quite the jest,
A grand parade of chaos, nature's fest.

Grace in the Granular Stillness

A grain of sand thinks it's a star,
"I'm destined for greatness, I've come so far!"
Glistening brightly in the sun's warm glow,
But next to a pebble, it feels rather low.

The waves roll in with a grand old laugh,
"Fancy a ride? Just take a path!"
While starfish lounge with such great poise,
Saying, "Life's a beach, find your joys."

Crabs scuttle sideways, thieves of the show,
Hoarding shell treasures, stack in a row.
The seaweed sways, calling it dance,
While shells whisper secrets of a lost romance.

In stillness, grace dances in delight,
Even the moon finds reasons to write.
Nature's humor spreads wide and free,
In every crevice, a whimsical spree.

The Lament of the Lost Traveler

Once a traveler, with map in hand,
Took the wrong turn in a foreign land.
As the sun blazed on, he scratched his head,
"Is that a mirage, or am I misled?"

With a sandwich left, and coffee long gone,
He sang to the cacti, found they weren't fun.
"Hey, little succulents, do you know the way?
Or are you just waiting for a sunny day?"

A tumbleweed rolled, laughing on cue,
"Take my advice, it's the least I can do!"
While lizards snickered from rocks up above,
The traveler sighed, "I need me some love!"

Adventures are wild, or so they say,
Especially when lost on a sunny day.
With a grin, he struts, his spirit still high,
For every mishap brings forth a new sky.

Shifting Grain Beneath the Stars

Underneath the twinkling light,
Grains wiggle left and right.
A dance for ants, a shadow show,
Stars wink, while we lay low.

Beneath the cosmos, grains take flight,
With little creatures, worlds in sight.
What a party, but where's the beer?
Guess we'll just spin in playful cheer!

Nature's chaos, a playful play,
Grains gossip, what can they say?
"Did you see that star's great fall?"
"Wow, who knew they had a ball?"

A tumble, a giggle in the air,
While crickets sing without a care.
Under stars, the grains unite,
In a comedy of cosmic night.

Footprints Lost to Time

In the desert, we walk tall,
Leaving tracks that soon will fall.
A game of hide and seek with fate,
"Hey, foot, don't make us wait!"

Each step a tale, or so we think,
Watch them vanish, there's no ink.
Footprints chuckle as they flee,
Like they've got a better spree!

Time plays tricks, it loves to tease,
"Lost your shoes? Just aim to please!"
In this riddle, we roam wide,
Chasing footsteeps that hide and bide.

With every stride, there's laughter near,
As grains giggle, "Forget the fear!"
Though lost to time, our spirits shine,
In fleeting paths that intertwine.

A Monologue of Grit and Gloom

Once a grain with dreams so bold,
Lost it all, or so I've told.
Sitting here with grit and gloom,
Wishing for a dance or zoom!

"Oh, to roll and laugh all day,
But here I sit, just pass the hay.
Life's a trick, a grand charade,
In this quiet, magic's made."

Every crack and every seam,
Holds the tales of hopeful dreams.
We'll laugh at clouds with all our might,
While grains giggle at our plight.

So let them wander, let them stray,
While I'm the grain with much to say.
In humor found, the moon will rise,
With jokes to share beneath our skies.

Solace Beneath the Arid Sky

Under skies that crack and dry,
We find peace, oh me, oh my.
No water here, just grains so sly,
"Hey, everyone! Want to give it a try?"

In the quiet, dust takes flight,
Grains whisper secrets, out of sight.
Let's have fun beneath this dome,
Laughing grains, we are at home.

A lizard slips, then makes a dash,
Watch it go, oh what a splash!
In the stillness, joy we find,
With grains unbothered, antics blind.

Here's the wisdom of our jest,
Even in the heat, we're blessed.
So raise a toast with grains so high,
In every laugh, we'll learn to fly.

Twilight's Embrace in a World Alone

In dusk where the crickets sing,
A lonely bird can't find a wing.
The moon winks down, a bright balloon,
Chasing shadows with a laugh, too soon.

A solitary cat takes its stroll,
Meowing tales of a missing bowl.
It struts like royalty on the sand,
In a silent kingdom, so unplanned.

The stars giggle, gossip in space,
About a traveler lost in place.
With a map that's upside down and wrong,
He dances unaware, humming a song.

Yet in this hush, with jest and cheer,
Life's confetti falls from nowhere near.
So let's toast to friends who seem to roam,
In every corner, there's a little home.

Timeworn Paths of the Lonesome Traveler

A traveler drags his weary feet,
On paths where the tumbleweeds greet.
His suitcase is filled with old regrets,
And snacks he won't remember, bets.

Each step he takes, the ground does sigh,
"Where's your friend?" the wind will pry.
He shrugs and munches a crumbly snack,
Wonders if he's missed the train back.

A cactus winks, its smile discreet,
As if it knows the tales of defeat.
The traveler chuckles, adjusts his hat,
Maybe he's missing more than that.

Yet with each laugh, the miles rewind,
Leaving footprints, mischief aligned.
In every moment of solo plight,
He finds the joy in the fading light.

Breath of the Forgotten Oasis

In a place where mirages play tricks,
A sunburned frog does silly kicks.
It croaks a tune, the trees all bow,
To a dancer who's still figuring out how.

The palm trees lean in with gossiping leaves,
Whispering secrets where nobody sees.
"I swear I saw movement by the pool,"
A tiny lizard giggles, "Just a fool!"

A lost explorer, looking quite grand,
Cheers to himself with a poorly made band.
His song echoes, a melody strange,
In a forgotten oasis, where dreams rearrange.

But don't mind the laughter from the breeze,
Nature's humor brings travelers to their knees.
So sip from the fountain of silly vibes,
And lose yourself among carefree tribes.

Shadows Stretching in the Quiet Canvas

In twilight's glow, shadows start to play,
Painting pictures in a clumsy way.
A gopher peeks out, adjusting its tie,
In a world of quiet, adventures nearby.

The moon giggles as it stretches wide,
Across the canvas, where dreams abide.
As whispers of laughter fill the air,
It's a parade of silliness everywhere.

A random shoe left by the trail,
It tells of journeys that did not prevail.
Was it a runaway? Or just a trick?
The shadows snicker, "It's quite the pick!"

And when the stars begin to twinkle,
They poke fun at clouds that like to sprinkle.
In this whimsical night, so free and sly,
The shadows stretch, and life passes by.

Echoes of an Empty Horizon

A seagull squawked, it took a dive,
The empty beach tried hard to jive.
I threw a shell, it rolled away,
It whispered secrets of a dull day.

My shadow danced, it stole my hat,
The breeze just laughed, how rude is that!
Footprints claimed, yet sand's a trick,
They washed away, a magic flick.

A turtle snored, mistook my shoe,
For a cozy shell, oh what a view!
I watched him wiggle, snore and snore,
In this vast emptiness, who's keeping score?

The sun did set, a peachy hue,
Sipping on lemonade, just me and you.
But where are you? I sadly muse,
Oh well, I'll tell my shoes the news.

Embracing the Weight of Isolation

In solitude, I found my chair,
The wind said, 'Aren't you quite rare?'
I chuckled back, with a cheeky grin,
Oh yes, my friend, let the fun begin!

Talking to crabs, they chirped in tune,
Brought my shell headphones, listened to the moon.
But each crab pinched, what a nasty rhyme,
I'll just stick to the seagull mime.

An echo laughed from stones nearby,
"Why stay alone? Just ask, oh why!"
A cactus winked, it looked quite bold,
I replied, "You prickly thing, I'm sold!"

But laughter echoed—what a thrill!
In the weight of quiet, I found my will.
Was it isolation? Some would say,
I just call it a beach holiday!

In the Shadow of Ancient Rocks

Staring at rocks, I'm lost in thought,
What wisdom here? Why so distraught?
They stayed so still, a formidable crew,
While I made a joke, they stoned it too.

An ancient boulder rolled its eyes,
"If you want laughs, you need to rise!"
I tried to tumble, fell flat on my face,
The rocks all chuckled, "We know this place."

A goat offered wisdom, up on a ledge,
"Life's just a hike, keep up your pledge!"
So I joined him, hopping like a fool,
The journey's better when you break the rule.

In the shadow of giants, I felt quite small,
But never alone, with laughter in thrall.
A party of rocks, crabs, and my wit,
In this silly realm, I choose to sit.

Tides of Time in the Wasteland

Waves rolled in, a slosh and a splash,
Tickling my toes, oh what a clash!
I built a castle, it rose with pride,
Soon washed away, the tide deride.

The sun, a joker, played hide and seek,
Clouds puffed up, looking all meek.
I waved them hello, they waved back sweet,
I guess solitude can't handle defeat.

Seagulls auditioned, squawking their best,
A concert of chaos, no time for rest.
I threw them snacks; they took their bow,
"Okay, that's it! New talent is now!"

With laughs and quirks, the day slipped by,
In this quirky realm where time can lie.
So grab a seagull, or just a sea shell,
In this funny wasteland, all's well that's well.

Remnants of Solitary Journeys

A traveler stumbles, trips over air,
His shadow laughs, does not seem to care.
With pockets of dreams and a map upside down,
He searches for voices in a ghostly town.

The sun throws a party, the clouds crash the scene,
Making friends with the lizards, feeling quite green.
Waves of confusion in the bright golden light,
He dances with footprints, a comical sight.

A mirage offers coffee, but it's just a swirl,
The grains of the day tickle and whirl.
With each sip of sand, he chuckles aloud,
His laughter bounces, a whimsical crowd.

Oh, the birds start to giggle, and the cacti just grin,
As he waltzes on pathways where no one's been.
Remnants of journeys are stuffed in his shoes,
A treasure of folly, of laughs, and of blues.

Laments in the Dunes' Silence

In silence so loud, he tries to complain,
His only reply is the wind's subtle vein.
A tumbleweed tumbles, with a laugh oh so grand,
As it rolls on by, giving life some soft sand.

He yells at the grains, but they just sit still,
A stubborn brigade of the infinite mill.
With each empty echo, a punchline delayed,
His pillow of laughter, a grand serenade.

Cacti hold secrets, but none hold a joke,
While he wanders the quiet, the thirsting for smoke.
Each cry of a seagull, a satire so bright,
In the sun-soaked embrace of a soft, silly light.

And yet in the distance, a camel appears,
With sunglasses on, not bothered by fears.
They share in the giggles, a weird little duo,
In the sea of the quiet, they sing a funny show.

Footsteps Fading into Memory

He strolls through the echoes of dust and of time,
With each step dissolving, yet still feels sublime.
His shoes filled with whispers, a tune in the breeze,
Stomping on moments, just trying to tease.

The path starts to chuckle, a comedian's play,
While clouds above ponder their next big ballet.
With shadows of laughter, they dance in a line,
Chasing their tails like a well-worn design.

The footprints behind him fade with a smirk,
As he jigs to a tune where the lost spirits lurk.
Each grain has a tale, a slight in-joke,
Dancing on memories, as memories choke.

Yet as he keeps moving, he can't help but grin,
For every lost moment brings good times within.
He finds that the laughter will always stick around,
In every step taken, no matter the ground.

Hollow Requiem Beneath Starlit Skies

Beneath the vast canvas of night's lighted stare,
He strums on a ukulele, banishing care.
The shadows groove wildly, yet none make a sound,
As he croons to the stars, in a world unbound.

The moon giggles softly, a bright little tease,
While the planets all wobble, like they've had too much cheese.
He sings of lost socks and a forgotten shoe,
In the absurdity of joy, becoming anew.

Echoes of laughter are whispered around,
With comets that twinkle, and shoot with a bound.
Each sigh of the night carries humor untold,
And tales of the silly, in wonder they mold.

Yet, as dawn approaches, the giggles descend,
Twirling in courage, they, too, must bend.
He waves to the twilight, this hollowed-out time,
Finding bliss in the chaos, a rhythm, a rhyme.

Mirage of the Heart's Silence

In a desert where thoughts take a stroll,
I chased a mirage, lost my role.
It twinkled like laughter, and vanished so fast,
Left me with footprints and questions to cast.

A cactus gave me a wink and a grin,
'Hope you find water, you're in quite a spin!'
With tumbleweeds dancing, my thoughts take a leap,
Turns out that silence can be quite the heap.

Each grain of sand had a tale it would tell,
About dreams that go missing and wishes that fell.
I laughed at the echoes, so silly and bright,
In this vast, empty space, my heart learned to kite.

So I gather my thoughts like a quirky parade,
With jokes on the wind, I can't be afraid.
For laughter is gold in this quirky expanse,
And maybe the mirage just wants to dance.

Deserted Dreams in Endless Grains

In a land where dreams play hide and seek,
Endless grains giggle, feeling quite cheeky.
They whisper sweet nothings to the tired sun,
'Come join our party; we might even run!'

A lonely tumbleweed planned a surprise,
With a party for clouds, floating up in the skies.
But clouds, being shy, just puffed away fast,
Leaving tumbleweed laughing, with dreams unsurpassed.

Mirages sang jingles, with voices so clear,
I wondered if they could spike up my beer.
But alas, it was water, as dry as a bone,
Yet laughter can lighten even the stone.

So I danced through the grains, like a star on a spree,
With dreams in my pocket, and all things carefree.
For even in deserts where solitude lurks,
There's comedy hidden behind how it works.

The Stillness Between Heartbeats

In the stillness where nothing seems to move,
I heard my heart giggle, making its groove.
Right there between beats, a joke took its seat,
And laughter arose from a silence so sweet.

I wondered if crickets were keeping the score,
As time took a break, and dreams opened doors.
Thoughts wandered off, with nibbles of fun,
In this quirky stillness, I felt like I'd run.

Each heartbeat a chuckle, a sigh, and a cheer,
Telling tales of clouds that forgot how to steer.
In this pause, I found rhythm, surprisingly right,
Where stillness became a dance, shining bright.

So I twirled with the silence, on a journey so wide,
With humor my compass, my heart open wide.
And though time may tick softly, and moments take flight,

Laughter's a treasure, hidden deep in the night.

Last Light on the Abandoned Horizon

As the last light washed over the barren view,
I played peekaboo with shadows anew.
The sunset chuckled, tickling the breeze,
While wisdom winked from the tips of the trees.

A lone jackrabbit hopped, with style and delight,
Said, 'Join me, dear friend, in the fading light!'
We plotted our escape from the mundane day,
In a world full of giggles, come what may.

The horizon stretched wide, a canvas of dreams,
Where laughter could echo, or so it seems.
I scribbled my thoughts on a grain of bright dust,
And watched them take flight, just for my trust.

So with the last light, we danced through the night,
In a world so abandoned, we'd ignite pure light.
For even horizons can share in the fun,
And sometimes the end is just a new run.

The Prism of Solitude's Light

In a room full of joy, I found a lone sock,
Whispering stories of cozy old rock.
It danced 'round the floor like a lost little toy,
Chasing dust bunnies with giggles of joy.

The walls held their breath as it spun with grace,
With a flair for the silly, a comical space.
Twirling in solitude, strutting about,
That sock was the queen of a sock puppet rout.

A cereal box joined with a clatter and crash,
They held a grand party, a distinctive bash.
Imaginary friends filled the air with a cheer,
Though it's just me and my snacks, no one else here.

Laughter echoed, a symphony's tune,
With a box of old crayons and a paper moon.
To each little dance, a tune must be played,
In my room of reflections, where silliness swayed.

Refractions in a Grain of Time

A hitchhiker's thumb is stuck in the sand,
He thought he could catch a ride to a band.
But the only thing passing was a snail on a roll,
With dreams of a vacation to reach his goal.

Time's a sly trickster, just watch it divide,
It stretches and shortens like we're on a slide.
With a watch that just giggles and taunts with glee,
It's always 'o'clock' when you need a good spree.

The echo of laughter from a crack in the wall,
A party of shadows, they're having a ball.
While I sip on some soda, they turn up the beat,
Oh, the wildness of nothing—it's really quite neat!

Each tick is a tickle, each tock is a grin,
In the grain of the hourglass, where chaos begins.
So I ride on this whimsy, let time slip away,
With a wink and a nudge, here's to a funny day!

Veils of Dust over Untold Stories

Underneath the old bed, forgotten and grim,
Lie tales of old socks, sing in harmony's hymn.
Dust bunnies whisper of mischief and lore,
With giggles that echo from yesterday's door.

There's a shoe with a secret, a lacesome plot,
That yearns for adventures but sits here to rot.
Each step it might take, in the air it would prance,
Dreaming of stardust, it missed its grand chance.

A spider's web spun with a delicate thread,
Weaves stories of shoelaces that once freely fled.
With a flick of a feather, it dances in sight,
To pen down the tales of the absurd night.

So let's toast to the dust, let the stories unfold,
Of lonely old objects with antics untold.
The ghosts of my home have a laugh as they play,
In this whimsical world, where boredom won't stay.

The Allure of Endless Horizons

A cat on the windowsill, dreaming of space,
Where every new horizon's a silly new place.
With paws that are plotting and whiskers that twitch,
It yearns for a journey, a pounce, or a glitch.

The sunrise arrives, but the snooze button wins,
With pancakes for breakfast, and giggles begin.
Each yawn is a riddle, each stretch a parade,
In the kingdom of lazy, where naps never fade.

Chasing after butterflies, they jog and they prance,
But I'm deep in the couch, in a cozy romance.
While the world's full of wonders, I've set up a trap,
In the allure of horizons, I'm taking a nap.

So raise up a cheer for the whimsical quest,
Of cats, couch potatoes, and time spent at rest.
With every new dawn, let's just bask in the light,
As laughter is free and the sky is our flight.

Hushed Conversations with the Wind

The breeze whispered jokes, oh so sly,
Tickling the leaves and making them cry.
A squirrel rolled by, with a nut in its paw,
Laughing at clouds that had nothing in thaw.

The trees joined the chatter, all rustles and glee,
While shadows danced lightly, as happy as can be.
A tumbleweed chuckled, it spun with a twist,
Creating a ruckus, as if it were missed.

Each gust brought a giggle, a tickle of air,
Whispering secrets that vanish in flair.
An echo of chuckles that bounced from afar,
Sharing the humor, like a bright shooting star.

In the quiet of dusk, the wind took a bow,
Grateful for laughter, and the joy of the how.
So here in the stillness, remember to play,
For even the breezes have jokes on display.

The Luminescence of a Quiet Soul

In shadows, she giggled, her light like a tease,
As candles waxed funny, 'till they took a knee.
A glow worm named Larry was wearing a hat,
Dancing in circles, much too cute for that.

They tried to have meetings, those flickering lights,
But starlight kept floating, too busy for sights.
A comet gave wink that made everyone grin,
Spreading joy around while the party begins.

With laughter like lanterns, they lit up the night,
While friends from the cosmos brought snacks for the bite.
The echoes of chuckles, how sweet they would sway,
As dreams soared and swooped in a whimsical play.

So let your soul twinkle, embrace that weird glow,
For what's hidden quietly is the laughter we sow.
In the heart of the night, where silence is gold,
There's humor so bright, let your stories be told.

Threads of Silence in the Fabric of Time

A needle and thread stitched whispers of thought,
In patterns of silence, where laughter is caught.
Tick-tock went the clock, but the time took a break,
To share silly stories that made the stars quake.

At twilight, the tapestry shimmered and glowed,
With memories woven in jests overflowed.
An hourglass toppled, grains danced on the floor,
Each one a giggle that opened the door.

The fabric of moments, so soft and so bright,
Held laughter like secrets, that tickled the night.
As stitches unravel, let joy take its climb,
For humor is timeless, in this weave of rhyme.

So pull on those threads, and don't you delay,
Find joy in the quiet, and let spirits play.
In the loom of existence, trust the gentle design,
For life's little stitches, are where laughter aligns.

An Odyssey of Quiet Waters

The river partook in a giggle or two,
As fishes wore hats, and the frogs sang a tune.
A sailboat went drifting, caught wind of a jest,
While turtles debated who the fastest was best.

Beneath the still surface, a riddle was spun,
As ripples exchanged puns, oh what silly fun!
A group of wise otters played games with their tails,
While crickets composed, telling tall fables.

They splashed with abandon, like laughter on waves,
The current a chorus, that nudged and it swayed.
At dusk, when all quiet, the stars took their turn,
Shining down secrets, waiting for us to learn.

So ponder and chuckle, in waters so still,
For humor is flowing, a sweet little thrill.
An odyssey waits for those eager to glide,
In the laughter of currents, let joy be your guide.

www.ingramcontent.com/pod-product-compliance
Lightning Source LLC
Chambersburg PA
CBHW072132070526
44585CB00016B/1648